Leveraging ADP Payroll And The Work Number For Personal Financial Power

Corey P Smith

Library of Congress Catalog Card Number: On File

Library of Congress Control Number: On File

Printed in the United States of America

Editor: Chandra Sparks Taylor, www.chandrasparkstaylor.com
Cover design: Felix Walker
Book design: Essex Graphix, www.essexgraphix.com

The Credo Company
4466 Elvis Presley Blvd., Ste. 260
Memphis, TN 38116
coreysmith1793@gmail.com
www.coreypsmith.com

CONTENTS

DISCLAIMER

This publication is designed to provide accurate and authoritative information with regard to the subject matter covered. While all of the stories described in the book are based on true experiences, most of the names are pseudonyms, and some situations have been changed slightly for educational purposes and to protect each individual's privacy. It is sold with the understanding that the publisher is not engaged in rendering legal or other professional advice. If legal advice or other expert assistance is required, the services of a competent professional person should be sought.

AUTHORS STATEMENT

In 1990, I got hired at my first job. It was Kentucky Fried Chicken, and I can remember being so excited. Throughout the years of writing books on credit, I have talked about some of my life experiences and some of the lessons that I learned from my father and this story is no different.

However, I don't know who learned the greater lesson me or him. The reason that I was so excited about the job was because I began to think about all the possibilities that I would have now to buy whatever I wanted. You see my dad had already planted the seed in me that gave me the capacity to dream, but there was something that I missed in that lesson and that was the TIME that I would be trading for MONEY.

Once I started the job, I learned that lesson pretty fast and so I quit within a three-week time period. I can remember my dad telling me that he was so disappointed in me because I quit the job. He felt as though this might become a common practice that I would follow throughout my life. My dad was a hard worker and a man who had never quit anything in his life.

What my dad did not realize was that I was not quitting the job because I was a quitter, I was quitting the job because I was an observer that was able to process the outcome of other peoples circumstances based on daily routines that I observed them doing over and over again. That practice was working a job and making no progress because they were not being fairly compensated for their time. This feeling that I had was simply the boss in me waking up at an early age.

You see there is nothing wrong with working for someone else, but most of the time the only way that you are going to make progress in your life is that you must be fairly compensated for your time. The problem is that most people are not, but you have to make a decision early on about whether the paycheck that you are receiving is worth your time.

"If you show someone their future, they have no future.

You take away the mystery, you take away hope"

Michael Jennings

CHAPTER I

THE PAYCHECK TRAP

I want to explain how many people are conditioned to accept the paycheck trap that over ninety eight percent of Americans practice every day. They do not fully understand how the forty-hour work week slowly steals their life away from them and before they know it, they have completed that dash between birth and death.

Thinking about this, most people have to work forty hours a week and sometimes more considering overtime before they see one dime. And sometimes they are not even paid weekly, they are paid every two weeks.

You see this delay in money does nothing more than create an endless pattern of catching up and causing poor people to depend on loans, check advance businesses, credit cards and sad to say the pawn shop. Many of them find themselves with late fees and overdrafts. The way paychecks are setup it keeps people in a cycle of need and dependency.

Let me explain how this cycle is designed. Whoever you work for takes money from you before you see any of your paychecks. They take income taxes, Medicare, social security, insurance deduction and any money that you have being deducted for a retirement plan like 401k.

This is why there is an advantage to being a business owner, no matter how small the business is and even if you work a job. I will explain later. Business owners are in control of how they pay taxes and how they pay themselves.

There is something that I want you to consider. You ever notice how the cost of living has constantly risen while working wages have only increased by a small margin. People are paid almost the wages as they were ten years ago, but rent, groceries, gas prices, telephone and utility bills have continued to go up. This creates the rat race of living paycheck to paycheck with no way to save money.

Let's look at the term rat race. When all of your money is married to a job, you can't afford to take risks, start a business, miss work and definitely not quit. The paycheck is the cheese, the job is the treadmill, and you are the rat chasing the check every one or two weeks.

What many people do not realize is that companies create cashflow by making employees wait on their first paycheck either weekly or bi-weekly, creating an illusion in the minds of the employees making them believe the tradeoff is equal.

There has to be a bridge when you are living paycheck to paycheck and that bridge creates debt and that debt is a form of control. Anytime you depend on a paycheck, you depend on your credit and that entails credit cards, loans, payday loans, and rent to own. People who work are taxed the most and the highest, therefore trading time for money and never able to escape the rat race.

"I'm just here for the paycheck"

CHAPTER II

TRADING TIME FOR MONEY

In order for you to fully understand how this whole idea of working for a paycheck was created to steal your dream. I at least need to give you the back story. The one thing that you must understand is a paycheck is about control and not about financial freedom. The eight-hour workday wasn't created to help people prosper in life, it was created to stop exhausted workers from collapsing or dying on the job and making sure that they were productive at the same time.

You see, back in the 1800's people would work ten to sixteen hours a day for six days a week. Even children worked in the factories and sometimes would pass out from being so tired. This created movements like the Haymarket Affair of 1886. The

Haymarket Affair was an illusion if you ask me, because it basically was a movement where workers got eight hours to work, eight hours to sleep, and eight hours for the rest of their daily routines. Remember when I said the paycheck was a form of control.

Labor representatives were able to get some poorly enforced eight-hour workday laws on the books during this time, but it was Henry Ford who voluntarily implemented it in all of his automobile factories. Because he adopted the eight-hour workday, forty hours slowly became the accepted norm and in 1938 Franklin D. Roosevelt President of the United States passed the Fair Labor Standards Act making it a federal law. By making the eight-hour workday a federal law, it was simply a way of structuring our society for dependence, meaning the working class would still be controlled.

If you do not understand, let me explain. They basically duped people out of the majority of their lives. Think about it eight hours of sleep, eight hours of rest and eight hours for everything else. Although technology has changed a lot of things and we now have AI, the eight-hour format still remains the same. After most people work twenty-five or thirty years, they still end up broke with maybe a pen or gold watch.

"Seven out of ten Americans are one paycheck away from being homeless."

CHAPTER III

EVERYTHING AIN'T FAIR

Before I get into the meat and potatoes about The Work Number, there is one thing that everyone should know, and that is The Work Number is a consumer reporting agency in disguise.

The reason I say this is because The Work Number collects and sells employment and income data. Therefore, it is governed by the Fair Credit Reporting Act (FCRA). Which means that you have a legal right to your consumer file and a right to dispute any inaccuracies found within your Work Number consumer report.

But remember not everything is fair when it comes to the Fair Credit Reporting Act. Why do you say that Corey P Smith? I say that because even though you can dispute anything in your report The Work Number will not fix it because they do not create your employment data, your employer does. That means they will not correct any errors found in your report. They will only report what your employer sends.

When you submit a dispute, The Work Number will only forward that dispute to your employer and if the employer does not respond, the dispute will be terminated without any changes being made.

You see employment data is not like your credit report. The FCRA will sometimes enforce the three major credit bureaus differently than The Work Number. Your employer will not be penalized, and it would be difficult to sue them because of inaccurate reporting. The work Number will not take any accountability because they make money by selling your employment history and making corrections would cost them money and resources.

The goal of this book is to teach people how not to get trapped between The Work Number and their employer even if you have a job.

“Never confuse the size of your paycheck

with the size of your talents”

Marlon Brando

CHAPTER IV

WHO STOLE MY MONEY

It is not a crime to be poor, but the crime is how they trick poor people in impersonal and systematic ways where you cannot pin the crime on one individual person. What I mean by this is employers can program their computers to steal money from their employees in ways like showing up to work fifteen minutes before their shift.

Lenders like credit card companies and payday lenders steal money from the poor by charging insane interest rates such as companies like TBO Bank who charge a 300 percent interest rate on their loans only to create debt traps for its borrowers. And it is not just private companies; it is also the local governments. They trick the poor through fines, fees and court cost.

The reason I titled this Chapter "Who Stole My Money" was because most people are like small children attending school on an empty stomach. The only thing that child is thinking about is food and the only thing the poor and working class is focused on is money. They are focused on the things that they lack the most and that is money. I will explain later how this is done by keeping everyday people living paycheck to paycheck and controlling their time. You see the saying "Crime is Money" only make sense because of the financial gain that criminal's benefit from committing the crime, but the truth be told the most money is made in the punishment for the crime. The one thing that you have to remember is never take pride in your poverty because the only thing that makes the world go round is money and the role that these companies are connected to those people who have the power to punish. In a sense being poor pushes you to the criminal state of mind to get some money by any means necessary.

I am going to explain to you how ADP Payroll and The Work Number could be perceived as a scam. No, I do not mean these two companies are actually stealing money. However, they have created a system that implements a trap. This trap can be found in the way that they collect payroll data and how they sell it and how it is used as an economic weapon against poor people.

Let me explain how this works. Whoever you are employed by sends your payroll information to ADP and ADP Payroll in turn sends that information to The Work Number. The crazy thing about this, is most employees have no idea that their income, hours, start date, end date, employment status and even any judgments or garnishments are sent to The Work Number which is owned by Equifax. The other part of this trap is you the employee did not give them consent; your employer gave consent.

The one thing that you have to keep in mind is Equifax is in the business of collecting data and selling it. They sell your employment and payroll information to banks, debt collectors, landlords, car dealerships, government agencies and any company that is in the business of buying data. You have to remember they get paid every time any data associated with your name is pulled, but you don't get paid nothing.

Because Equifax owns The Work Number and they sell your payroll and employment history this actually is used as a weapon against you coupled with your credit history. This is double jeopardy because employers show your hours, how often you change jobs and any layoffs that you have, now compare this to the creditors that are using this to control your purchasing power because they can see all of this as well, because remember The Work Number sells your information.

The last thing that I want to point out about The Work Number is that unlike the three major credit bureaus, you cannot freeze, delete, block or remove anything from your Work Number file. This is the reason underwriters rely on it so much because it is an automated digital tool that can instantly verify any person that is applying for a loan income, payroll data, and employment data with one stroke of the key.

Keep in mind that Experian and TransUnion also own employment and income verification companies as well. Experian owns CCC Verify/Experian Verify and TransUnion has a partnership with Truework's, who also provides income and employment verification. The credit bureaus are leveraging their enormous data networks to verify employment and wages, and they are doing this by partnering up with payroll providers to streamline access to real time data. I have listed the top income and employment verification companies.

- The Work Number
- HireRight
- Checkr
- First Advantage
- s2Verify
- Truework
- Tenstreet
- Goodhire
- Mitratech (AssureHire)
- Truv

We all have an Economic Identity that is being created by The Work Number and when you couple this with ADP Payroll, it can lock us all into the same economic class, but once you understand how to navigate this system, you can use it to build your own employment record by reporting your own payroll. Therefore, controlling the economic narrative.

“I don’t miss the economic insecurity, the

living paycheck to paycheck”

Drew Carey

CHAPTER V

THE POWER OF PAYROLL

It is one thing to get a paycheck, and it is another thing to sign the paycheck. Most entrepreneurs understand the hustle of becoming a business owner, but many still do not see it through to the point where they are signing the paychecks. In this chapter I will talk about how payroll is the missing piece that connects entrepreneurship to financial leverage, and this structured income system is what rich people have used for decades.

You must understand that The Work Number is a huge database owned by Equifax that collects income and employment history for over three million companies. It is the go-to for banks, auto dealers and mortgage lenders because they can verify income instantly. ADP Payroll is a big reason for this because they are one of the biggest clients of The Work Number.

Do not worry, by the time you get finished reading this book you will understand how ADP Payroll updates your payroll and how lenders pull this information. You see most business owners pay themselves incorrectly and leave no verifiable paper trail. First you must understand that W-2 income is more trusted than 1099 and creating a payroll will show financial stability to any underwriter.

The first rule to this game is consistency. Do not sabotage yourself with skipping payrolls, not withholding taxes and salary fluctuations. Underwriters will always look at job titles, start date, year to date income, pay frequency and pay rate. If any of these things are inconsistent it will cause a red flag. You want to run your payroll for at least six months.

You cannot have a worker mentality; you must have a boss mentality because a work mentality will create dependency and put a limit on your ability to gain real financial power. Do not allow your identity to be tied to a paycheck and job titles. Have a boss mentality because it will keep you focused on building leverage through assets, investments and controlling your time and not laboring for someone else. Do not be the person that always ask the question "How much do I get paid per hour?" Be the person who is trying to come up with a way to make money while you sleep.

Owners build systems that use other people's time, money and intelligence. They understand by doing this the system can work without them being present. At the end of the day workers chase checks and owners cut checks.

Let me just say that I understand that everybody cannot be rich because the world needs workers and not wealthy people. The reason why is because if everybody was rich the system would collapse. This is why school teaches you how to function in a job capacity and not how to build wealth. Wealth requires a lot of things such as risk, failure, pressure and delayed gratification.

Most people are content with comfort. People who truly entrepreneurs understand how to monetize information, leverage debt and buy assets. On the other hand, poor people trade their time for a time clock.

“Make Your Passion Your Paycheck”

CHAPTER VI

SETTING UP ADP PAYROLL

I always like to talk about the history of any company that I am writing about, and ADP is no different. It was first called Automatic Payrolls, Inc. (API) when Henry Taub founded it in 1949 as a manual payment service for local companies in New Jersey. He was later joined by his brother Joe Taub and a salesman by the name of Frank Lautenberg. In 1957 the company invited technology by switching to punch cards and mainframes and changing its name to Automatic Data Processing, Inc.

I want to be very clear and simple in explaining how to set up your ADP Payroll profile in order for smooth integration with The Work Number. You must remember that the only way to get your income into The Work Number is by using a payroll provider. The top three are ADP, Paychex, and Paycom, with ADP being the largest.

Let me stress three things you want to pay yourself as a W-2 employee, make sure you are withholding the proper taxes and enroll your company with The Work Number, once this is done, they will update your information every payroll cycle. Remember even if you are the business owner, you want to pay yourself as a W-2 employee, this is the best way to verify income as opposed to a 1099.

The first thing you want to do is choose the right ADP product and I say this because they have multiple products and choosing the wrong payroll product could cause reporting problems with The Work Number. I have listed the options below:

-ADP Run (best option for small businesses)

It is designed to grow with a business, from basic payroll needs to more comprehensive HR support.

-ADP Workforce (mid-size companies)

It helps companies manage everything from onboarding to retirement, offering self service for employees and managers via web and mobile, and simplifying compliance and data management.

-ADP TotalSource (Professional Employer Organization-PEO)

It handles complex HR tasks like payroll benefits, compliance, and hiring, while giving owners time back to focus on their business. It works through a co-employment model, offering expert HR support, access to better benefits, tax administration, and technology, all under one platform.

-Roll By ADP (mobile companies)

Designed specifically for very small business owners, using a conversational, chat-based interface to simplify running payroll, paying employees (direct deposits, checks), calculating and filing taxes, and managing basic HR tasks with minimal experience needed and employee self-service.

When you sign up for ADP Payroll you want to have all of these things in front of you because you will be asked to enter them, and I have listed them below as well.

- Legal business name (as shown on EIN documentation)
- EIN Number
- Entity type
- Business address
- State tax registration numbers (for withholding unemployment tax)
- Secretary of State Control Number
- NAIC Code for your company's industry

You will also be asked to provide your business bank routing, account number and verification because ADP uses two withdrawals and that is Payroll funding and Tax liability payments. ADP will also ask that you determine how often your employees will be paid and the payment types. This just simply means weekly, bi-weekly, semi-monthly or monthly and the payment types will consist of hourly, salary, commissions and bonuses.

After you have done all of this, the next step will be entering your employees or contractors' personal information into the ADP Payroll system. You will need to provide the following information listed below:

- Social Security Number
- Residential Address
- Date of Birth
- W-4
- Banking Information for Direct Deposit

If you have contractors that you are paying, you will need to provide the following information that is listed below:

- Name
- EIN/Social Security Number
- Residential Business Address

- Payrate
- Bank Information

The next step is very important when setting up your ADP Payroll and that is turning on your tax filing. Your tax filing information will be the following:

- Federal Taxes
- State Taxes
- Local Taxes
- Unemployment Insurance taxes
- W2s and 1099

Remember when I told you that lenders and underwriter can see how long that you have been working and even if you have been laid off. That is because the final step with setting up your ADP Payroll before running a test payroll run is configuring your time tracking. The options that you will have are listed below:

- ADP Time and Attendance
- Third-Party

- Manual

For those of you who do not know "third party" time tracking refers to using a time tracking system of software developed by a vendor other than ADP to record employee work hours. And "manual" means employees or managers directly enter of adjust hours (like on a spreadsheet or in the system) instead of the system automatically clocking them in/out via a time clock or app.

There is one part of this process that is called onboarding. When you do your onboarding for ADP there is a section for form I-9, or Employment Eligibility Verification. This is a section that you need to pay very close attention to because it gives you the option to allow ADP to immediately report your employment eligibility to The Work Number.

For those of you who do not understand how important the I-9 form is, then let me explain. As the employer you are attesting to the status of the employee, meaning you viewed documents proving identity and work authorization. It also requires you the employer to keep a list of acceptable forms (e.g. U.S. Passport, Drivers License and Social Security Card) on file for three years after the hire date or one year after termination. This is the reason; it is also important that you register your company with The Work Number in order to pull files on people that you plan on hiring. It is all about the appearance of looking bigger than what your company really is on paper.

After you have completed all of these steps you can (go live and run your first payroll. When you do your first test payroll ADP will pay your employees, withhold taxes, and update to The Work Number.) Run a test payroll to make sure the calculations, deductions, direct deposits and tax previews are correct. You always want to make sure that you are maintaining compliance. That means updating employee information, confirming tax filings, reviewing each payroll run and managing onboarding and offboarding. I have provided an example below to show you what employment verification letter should look like.

Hi ,

LLC is all set up with ADP Employment Verification, an automated service powered by The Work Number® an Equifax business. This service instantly and securely answers requests for your employees' employment and income information, such as when they apply for a loan, line of credit or government assistance. Lenders or government agencies may also verify the employee is qualified to continue to receive a benefit, collect a debt or enforce other obligations undertaken by the employee.

Your Employer Code is:

Please keep record of this code in the event it's needed for customer support.

Your employer code helps credentialed lenders, property managers, creditors, government agencies and others request your employees' employment and income information on www.theworknumber.com. Your employees can also use your employer code to see what information is shared about them when verification is requested.

To learn more about how you and your employees can make most of this service, visit www.theworknumber.com/sbs-ev-support. We encourage you to bookmark this webpage, which includes helpful resources including a handy poster to hang in your workplace that explains the service.

We're happy to help with any questions - just reach out when you need us!

Thank you,

Your ADP Employment Verification Team
SBSEVsupport@theworknumber.com
855-226-6779

For payroll or account-related questions, contact your regional ADP Service Center.

Always Designing for People™

“They never pay the slaves enough so they can get free, just enough so they can stay alive and come back to work”

Charles Bukowski

CHAPTER VII

THE WORK NUMBER

The origin of The Work Number dates back to the late 1980s when the profit potential associated with manual employment verification were slow and inefficient, so in 1985 the Talx Corporation now known as Equifax launched The W ork Number to automate income and job data for third party lenders. When you apply for a loan or a job, you typically sign a consent form. The "verifier" (e.g. bank or background check company) uses this consent to log in to The Work Number and download your data.

Now that you understand how to set up ADP Payroll, it is time to learn how to set up The Work Number (TWN), which is an Equifax owned company that verifies income and employment. Their database is utilized by banks, auto lenders, mortgage lenders, credit card companies, employers that are trying to verify past employment history and government agencies such as SNAP, IRS and Medicaid.

The first thing to remember is that your employer will upload your payroll data to The Work Number either weekly, bi-weekly or monthly. You as an employee will never be able to activate this automation unless you are the employer. Think about that last statement.

Since you are the employer, you will visit theworknumber.com/solutions/employer and click on "Get Started" business enrollment. You want to have all of your business information in front of you before you get started.

Next it will prompt you to put in the name of your company EIN number, the number of employees that you have and who your payroll provider will be. This is when you choose ADP, Paychex, or Gusto.

The last thing that you will do is choose your verification types, you can choose employment only or employment plus income. After that you can choose employee access.

First, they must go to employee.theworknumber.com and then click "Log In" or "Sign Up." After that they will enter their employer code which will consist of six digits. The next thing they must do is verify their identity by providing the last four of their social security number and date of birth. When these steps are completed, they will be able to create a username and password. This will allow them access to their profile.

After the entire setup is complete, banks, credit card companies, mortgage lenders and government agencies can verify information instantly. This means they can verify earnings history and generate salary keys.

I have provided an example of how you should fill out the signup form below.

⚠

PERSONAL DATA ASSISTANCE IS NOT AVAILABLE THROUGH THIS FORM

This form is intended to serve businesses only.

To view your personal information contained in The Work Number database, freeze your data, or submit a data dispute, please visit our Employees section.

Sign Up to Access Verifications for Your Business

Home / Account / Sign Up / Register

Start the verification process

To purchase verification reports, through our pay-as-you-go eCommerce channel, please complete this form. The information you provide will go through a rapid, thorough credentialing process. After credentialing is completed, you can log in and start using our verification service.

All fields are required.

How often do you expect to purchase verifications?

- (●) 1 to 2 verifications per week
- ( ) 1 to 2 verifications per month
- ( ) 1 to 2 verifications per year

Tell Us About Your Organization

Tell Us About Yourself

Tell Us About Your Verification Purchasing Needs

All fields are required.

Background Investigation - Pre Employment Screening

Why do you typically need to purchase verifications?

Employment purposes - Pre-employment/Hiring

Note: Equifax Workforce Solutions provides consumer report solutions, such as The Work Number and, in certain verifier industries, Smart Screen. Therefore, a permissible purpose is required under the FCRA.

Describe in detail how your organization will use this data. A minimum of 10 characters required.
The more details you provide, the quicker we can process your application.

Our company will use pre-employment verification information obtained through The Work Number solely for permissible employment related purposes, in compliance with the Fair Credit Reporting Act (FCRA) and all applicable federal and state laws.

Where will you access, order, and maintain the verification data?
Please enter the address where you work the majority of the time. We need to confirm this for security reasons.

☑ Same as my organization headquarters

Street Address — Working from Home?

1234 Robin Hood Lane

Apt/Suite

City

Memphis

State

Tennessee

Zip Code

38111

Do you plan to resell verification information to another party? — Mortgage Broker?

- ( ) Yes, I plan to resell this information to a third party
- (●) No, I plan to use this verification for my organization

☑ **By signing up, you acknowledge that this is a paid service offered to businesses.** You also acknowledge Equifax Workforce Solutions ("EWS") will conduct its required credentialing and vetting searches on the applying organization and applicant, which include criminal history checks among other searches. Customers must meet EWS credentialing requirements in order to request verifications.

To see your own employment record, you need to access your "Employment Data Report" (EDR).

1. Visit the Website: Go to theworknumber.com and select "Log In" followed by "View My Data".
2. Find Your Employer Code: You will often need an employer code to register. If you do not know it, you can search for your employer by name during the signup process. Common codes are often available on company intranets or by searching "company name plus employment verification" online.
3. Verify Identity: You will likely need to provide personal details (social security number, address, date of birth) and may need to verify via email or phone.

Once logged in, you can see exactly what verifiers see: your past job titles, tenure, and pay-by-pay income history. If you need a proof of employment letter for a landlord or a visa application, you can often generate an immigration or "employment summary" letter directly from the portal. This is often faster than waiting for your HR department to draft a manual employment letter.

Now keep in mind that The Work Number is governed by the Fair Credit Reporting Act (FCRA). If you decide to freeze your data, verifiers will receive a 'blocked" message when they try to access your file. They will then have to ask you to unfreeze it or provide manual documentation (like paystubs or a W-2).

According to privacy advocates and user reports, you have three main methods to request a freeze:

1. By Phone: Call The Work Number Client Service Center (listed as 866-222-5880). Select the option for "disputes" or "report an error" to reach a representative.
2. By Email: Send a request to twnfreeze@equifax.com. You will likely need to send proof of identity via a secure email channel they provide.
3. By Mail: Send a written request with proof of identity to Equifax Workforce Solutions (ATTN: Employment

Data Freeze) 3470 Rider Trail S, Earth City, MO. 63045.

Keep in mind that freezing your report does not delete the data, it only stops third parties from viewing it without your specific permission.

The information that I have given you up until this point about blocking and freezing your employment and income data is so important because this book is about controlling your income, especially if you have good credit. The reason why is because a common fear is that freezing your report will hurt your ability to buy a house, get a loan or buy a car. This is a misconception. You do not need to leave your data permanently exposed to get a loan. If your report is frozen and a lender needs access, you can generate a Salary Key (or a one-time access code) with The Work Number portal. You provide this single use code to the specific lender, allowing them to view your data once without unfreezing your report for the rest of the world. This gives you granular control over who sees your financial life and when they can see it.

The Work Number is the “credit report” of your career. While it offers convenience for income verification letter requests and loan approvals, it also represents a significant aggregation of your personal data. By logging in, reviewing your employment record, and understanding your right to freeze the data, you can take control of your professional narrative. I will leave you with this, it is all about the data. The more data that the credit bureaus collect on you, the easier it is to create effective machine learning algorithms because it allows models to learn patterns better and recognize human behavior. ALGORITHMS ARE USED TO PREDICT EVERYTHING, EVEN YOU!

“When I Was Young, People Lived Paycheck to Paycheck. Today, It Seems Like They Live From Credit Card Payment To Credit Card Payment”

Robert Kiyosaki

CHAPTER VIII

THE PLAID AND THE WORK NUMBER TRAP

Many people do not know what Plaid is or how it functions. Well, I am going to explain it to you and tell you how it integrates with The Work Number in order to create a trap when it comes to income verification.

Plaid is a financial technology company that acts as a secure middleman, connecting your bank accounts to various apps (like Venmo, Chime, Atlas and Robinhood), so you can easily link then and share data such as balances and banking transactions without sharing actual bank login credentials.

Remember The Work Number shows your payroll data, every paycheck amount, hours worked, overtime, YTD income, start and termination dates. Well banks will cross-check your Work Number information with Plaid. If anything does not match, the system triggers an automatic denial or fraud investigation.

The one thing that you have to remember about Plaid is that it shows ACH direct deposits, the dates and amounts of deposits and the employer deposit sources. By comparing this with The Work Number pay frequency, YTD income, bank deposits and paystubs the system eliminates any possible way to manipulate your income and employment.

This system is so powerful that it is impossible to create fake paystubs and fake bank statements. The people that it affects the most are poor and working-class people living paycheck to paycheck.

“Having Money Doesn’t Necessarily Make You Happy, But Not Having To Worry About Money Can Make You Very Happy”

CHAPTER IX

THE ONE DOLLAR SECRET

Have you ever heard of Business owners paying themselves a dollar and asked yourself, what is the benefit in that? Well let me explain. If you want to avoid the tax trap just because you make a lot of money, then you want to pay yourself one dollar.

The most heavily taxed form of income are people with high salaries. You see when you get a paycheck from a job, before you even see one dollar, you are hit with taxes. Think about it, they immediately take out federal income taxes, state income taxes, social security, Medicare, and sometimes payroll taxes. Well CEO's who pay themselves a one-dollar salary eliminate any taxes being deducted and they shift their wealth into assets.

Many people have never heard of Preferred Stock. Let me explain, most rich people or owners will pay themselves one dollar in salary and take the rest of their money in Preferred Stock. Preferred Stock gives owners priority in profits, payouts, liquidation, voting power and dividends. This is basically a wealth vehicle not a paycheck.

The reason they take the Preferred Stock is because they can borrow against it and therefore, they cannot be taxed on it because it is debt. The IRS cannot tax you on debt. Rich people use this method to get access to millions of dollars tax free. This method is called the Buy, Borrow, and Die method.

This is different from them selling their stock, because selling their stock would be considered a taxable event. You want to have a boss mentality, borrow instead of spending your own money. Remember in my book "Conspiracy of Credit" when I said, "You Can Borrow a Million Dollars, Faster Than You Can Make It Working A Job."

Everything that I have ever talked about is Wealth Strategies. Shelf corporations, business credit, ADP Payroll strategy, and borrowing against Intellectual Property are all from the Philosophy Own Nothing, But Control Everything.

www.ingramcontent.com/pod-product-compliance
Lightning Source LLC
LaVergne TN
LVHW022315200926
848481LV00004B/1351